Pemb[ury Library]

Tel Fax

pemburylibrary@kent.gov.uk

KT-558-467

02110 PCM

2 2 SEP 2010   2 0 NOV 2012

- 1 DEC 2010

2 5 JAN 2013

- 4 JUN 2011

- 8 MAY 2012   1 2 APR 2013

WITHDRAWN 1 2 JUL 2013

2 0 SEP 2012

1 4 AUG 2019

3 0 MAY 2012

Please return on or before the latest date above.
You can renew online at www.kent.gov.uk/libs
or by phone 08458 247 200

CUSTOMER SERVICE EXCELLENCE   Libraries & Archives

Kent
County
Council

C153852282

Professor Michael J Benton – dinosaur consultant
Valerie Wilding – educational advisor
Ben Newth – researcher

Scholastic Children's Books,
Euston House, 24 Eversholt Street,
London NW1 1DB, UK

A division of Scholastic Ltd
London ~ New York ~ Toronto ~ Sydney ~ Auckland
Mexico City ~ New Delhi ~ Hong Kong

First published in the UK by Scholastic Ltd, 2003
(as *Now You Know: T.rex – the dinosaur with the stupid smile*)
This edition published 2010

Text copyright © Helen Greathead, 2003
Illustrations copyright © Mike Spoor, 2003

ISBN 978 1407 11462 0

All rights reserved

Printed in the UK by CPI Bookmarque, Croydon, CR0 4TD

2 4 6 8 10 9 7 5 3 1

The right of Helen Greathead and Mike Spoor to be identified as author and illustrator
of this work respectively has been asserted by them in accordance with the Copyright,
Designs and Patents Act, 1988.

This book is sold subject to the condition that it shall not, by way of trade or otherwise
be lent, resold, hired out, or otherwise circulated without the publisher's prior consent in
any form of binding or cover other than that in which it is published and without a similar
condition, including this condition, being imposed on a subsequent purchaser.

Contents

Introduction **5**

T. rex outside your window **6**

T. rex is a big head **14**

T. rex eats – a lot **32**

T. rex grows up and UP and UP! **46**

T. rex has the last laugh **58**

Dino News **65**

Quizzes! **72**

Index **79**

Introduction

Dino names are often hard to say. It's easier to say Tyrannosaurus rex in bits:

Tie-ran-oh-sore-us rex

Bit of a mouthful, isn't it? Luckily, this dinosaur has a nickname.
You can call it T.rex
for short.

T.rex outside your window

Imagine this is your house. Your bedroom is here.

You're doing some homework. You look out of the window and see …

A Tyrannosaurus rex smiling
in at you.

T.rex was one of the biggest, scariest, meat-eating creatures that EVER lived!

Titchy arms →

You can see it had:

- thumping great legs – it could walk a long, long way to find food
- a huge, fat tail – to balance its heavy head and body
- titchy arms – for, er … well, nobody really knows what they were for.

Huge, fat tail

Thumping great legs

And you can see T.rex had a head that was just a bit bigger than you are. You'd fit nicely inside those jaws. So it's a good job you weren't around when T.rex lived!

The smile on its face made T.rex look a bit stupid, but those teeth were no joke. They were huge and sharp, and ready for action.

T.rex is a big head

T.rex might have looked a bit stupid, but it was actually a bit of a smarty pants. T.rex had a great big brain – for a dinosaur. But its brain wasn't all that much bigger than your dad's – take a look:

Your dad's brain

T.rex brain

And a brainy dinosaur wasn't brilliant at literacy and numeracy. T.rex needed a great big brain to make it good at seeing, hearing and smelling.

T.rex brain

This bit for smelling

This bit for seeing

This bit for hearing

T.rex carried its brain in its great big head. A T.rex skull was so big, it had to have holes, or "windows", so the head wasn't too heavy for its neck.

Windows

Some dinos had eyes on the sides of
their heads, like horses do today.
They could see if a creature
was creeping up
behind them.

But T. rex had
eyes like yours ...

… its eyes looked straight ahead.
This meant that T. rex could see
very clearly.
It could quickly
work out exactly
how far away a
creature was. So
when T. rex decided
to pounce … it
didn't miss!

Of course T. rex couldn't read or write, but most scientists think it could hear brilliantly. And they think it could make noises.

T. rex listened out for dinos it might like to eat. Vegetarian dinosaurs often moved about in herds. They called to each other to keep the herd together.

One T. rex could hear another T. rex calling, too.

But even more important than seeing or hearing was smelling. And T. rex had a *very* big nose.

With its incredible nose, T. rex could:

• sniff out creatures that were already dead – so it didn't have to bother killing them

- sniff out creatures that were alive, then kill and eat them
- sniff out T.rexes from another pack – and keep out of their way. They *weren't* friends!

Sniff! Sniff!

T.rexes usually
lived in small
groups, or packs.
The pack liked its
home to be as
stinky as possible.
That way other
creatures would know
this was their land
and *leave them
alone*!
Where did the smell
come from? Well, they
weren't too good at
clearing up. The nest
ponged of wee, poo
and sick!
And that's
not all …

... T.rex had bad breath, too!

Rotten bits of meat got stuck between its teeth. Wherever T.rex went a cloud of flies came, too. The flies fed on the smelly meat. Yuk!

Ever heard of a leech? It's a type of worm that lives on blood. Leeches lived inside a T.rex mouth. Maybe they gave T.rex terrible toothache – because a pterosaur (ter-oh-sore) could poke its beak inside those great jaws to pick out the leeches. And T.rex *wouldn't* bite its head off!

T.rex teeth were this big:

And there were *loads*
of them.

The teeth had edges like a
saw to cut through flesh easily!

Meat stuck to these jagged
edges and didn't slide off again.

The teeth were
shaped like this
across the middle:

They were nice
and strong for
chomping through bones.

They might break on a very
crunchy bone! But each T.rex
tooth had a spare. When one
broke another grew in its place.

T. rex had a stupid-looking smile for a reason. Its teeth curved backwards, so they didn't meet like this:

Instead, they overlapped like this:

Those T. rex teeth cut easily into an animal's flesh – they worked a bit like a pair of scissors. And because the teeth were curved, they kept hold of the flesh and didn't let go!

Before

There wasn't much left over after T.rex had eaten a meal. Except the really big bones – and a mush of leaves and shoots from the veggie dino's tum.

After

T.rex would eat just about *anything* – anything but its greens!

T.rex eats – a lot

For T.rex, some dinos were tastier than others.

A nice meaty Edmontosaurus (ed-mon-toe-sore-us) was a BIG treat. But it wasn't always easy to catch one.

Edmontosaurus was almost as big and heavy as T.rex.

It travelled in huge herds – if there were lots of them, bigger creatures might not dare to attack.

T.rex

Edmontosaurus

They could call to each other using a special skin pocket on their nose. It blew up like a balloon to make the sound!

Skin pocket
blown up

They could move quite fast – if they had to. But ...

… Edmontosaurus couldn't run for long, it was too big! And moving with the herd slowed it down.

It didn't have sharp teeth or claws for defending itself. A group of T. rexes could knock down Edmontosaurus easily.

There were always some weak animals in the herd. They might be sick, or they might be very young – T. rex picked on them first. Why bother running after an animal that could move fast?

A group of hunting T. rexes moved slowly, looking around and listening all the time. But they didn't attack until their leader gave the signal. Then …

... CHARGE!

One T.rex would run at
an Edmontosaurus with its jaws open
extra wide. It would take a ginormous
bite out of the thin Edmontosaurus neck.
The Edmontosaurus would fall to the
ground quickly. Lunch was ready!

When it came to eating, it was every creature for itself. And there was plenty of fighting over who got the juiciest bits.

But even T. rex wasn't terrifying all the time. It had to lie around for ages letting its food go down. After one Edmontosaurus lunch, T. rex might not eat again for six weeks!

T.rex liked to eat Triceratops (try-serra-tops), too, but they were harder to catch. Why? Because Triceratops *could* fight back. Its head had three long, sharp horns. And T.rex was scared of getting hurt! A wound from one of those horns could kill a T.rex – slowly and horribly.

So … T.rex tried to attack at night, when the herd was tired. At night, T.rex could see better than Triceratops. With luck, it wouldn't be spotted.

Spot the T.rex

But sometimes Triceratops did see T. rex. Then it would charge with its head down, and its horns pointing straight in front. It would aim for T. rex's tummy. And T. rex – possibly the scariest creature of all time – would turn and run away!

Triceratops

Some T. rexes preferred to live alone.
There was no chance of a tasty
Triceratops for them. Instead they might
chase a fast-moving Parksosaurus
(parks-oh-sore-us). This dinosaur was
just a bit taller than your dad. The
perfect size to feed one hungry T. rex.

Parksosaurus

T. rex

Different dinos tried different ways to save themselves from T. rex.

Some tried standing still. They hoped the patterns on their skin would hide them.

But T. rex could sniff them out.

Some tried running in zig-zags. T.rex could move quite fast over short distances, but the zig-zags might confuse it.

And T.rex had to be careful when it ran. Careful not to trip up …

Imagine T. rex is running across a hard patch of ground. It's running as fast as it can.

There's a large tree root lying across its path.

T. rex spots it too late. And falls to the ground ...

... CRRRAAASSSHHH!

T.rex was heavy. It held its
head quite high off the
ground. If it fell, its arms
were too tiny to break its
fall. It would land on its
tummy and wallop its head
on the ground, hard. T.rex would almost
certainly die!

Life wasn't easy for T.rex. Tripping up
was just one danger of being so big.
And a smaller T.rex had plenty more to
be scared of …

T.rex – grows up and UP and UP

This little dinosaur looks quite cute, doesn't it?

Ahhh!

But don't even think about picking it up for a cuddle! This is a baby T.rex and it can BITE!

When it hatched out, a baby T.rex was all covered in feathery fuzz. It was surprisingly small, and it soon got moving! Baby T. could stand up on its wobbly legs when it was only a few minutes old. And just a few hours later it would be toddling around the nest.

Grown-up T. rexes would bring food
for the baby. But its teeth were already
sharp and strong. Strong enough
to snap up any small creature
that got in its way.

Snap!

A baby T. rex lived
with a pack of five or six
grown-ups. They all followed
the lead of the biggest, scariest
dinosaur … which could be the baby's
mum! Female dinosaurs were usually
bigger than males, so they made all the
big decisions: when to move, when to
feed, when to rest, that sort of thing.

But sometimes the other T. rexes
thought they could lead the pack better.

The leader had to be on her
guard all the time.

Baby T. had to learn to get tough,
quickly.

Here's what Baby T. needed to watch out for:

- other dinosaurs might attack and kill it
- it might catch a disease and die
- it might get injured and die of its wounds
- it might even get eaten by another T. rex!

Imagine these baby T. rexes all hatched out together. Having so many brothers and sisters looks like fun, doesn't it?

But one year later, there might be only three of them left.

And a year after that, there might be only one baby left!

Not surprising they grew up to be so mean, is it?

The two-year-old T. rex wasn't much taller than its dad's kneecaps. And it had already lost all its fuzz. It still had big round eyes and a long, thin snout. And it wasn't big and heavy like its parents, so it could run a lot faster than them. It was ready to go off with the pack.

Eight years old

Two years old

Dad

At eight years old T. rex was almost as long as its dad but it was still skinny and fast. Now it had full-sized teeth that could cut through meat as easily as its dad's teeth did.

At 12 years old T. rex was fully grown. It might have a go at challenging the leader. Why not? It was big enough and heavy enough now – and fed up of being pushed around, too! There were a few things it could do:

1 Have a staring competition, like this:

Whoever turned away first was the loser.

2 Have a head-butting competition, like this:

Whoever turned away first was the loser.

3 Have an all-out fight,
like this:

Whoever *died* first was the loser!

A T.rex fight was not a pretty sight!
One dinosaur snapped its jaws round the
other's neck and kept biting. Then the
rest of the pack got in on the act … and
ate the loser!

So getting to be a grown-up T.rex was tough. But how long would it survive?

It's possible that the T.rexes that did survive just kept growing and growing. As they got older ...

... their eyes grew narrower ...

... their noses grew thicker ...

... lumpy horns grew over their eyebrows (great for head-butting contests) ... and they got heavier.

A lucky
T. rex might live
to be well over 100
years old, very slowly getting bigger and
bigger all the time.

T.rex has the last laugh

Scientists know about dinosaurs from looking at fossils. Fossils are bones or traces of dinosaurs, like a footprint or a tail trail, that have turned to rock over millions of years. Fossils can be very hard to find!

There's a place called Hell Creek, in Montana, North America. Over 100 years ago, a dinosaur expert called Barnum Brown went there to dig for dinos and he found the first T. rex skeleton, EVER.

Henry Fairfield Osborn studied the skeleton and called it Tyrannosaurus rex. It means, "king of the tyrant lizards".

A tyrant is someone who is cruel and nasty. So the name suited T. rex down to the ground!

Since
then only
20 T. rex
skeletons have
been found in the
whole world. And only
three of them have
skulls with all the
bony bits in place.

The most famous T. rex
skeleton is called Sue – after Sue
Hendrickson, who discovered her.
Sue's the biggest and the
most complete T. rex
skeleton *ever* found. And
she's worth megabucks!

If you go to America, you can visit Sue
at the Field Museum of Natural History
in Chicago. The museum bought Sue to
attract visitors, and so that its scientists
could study her.

From looking at her skeleton, the
scientists have worked out things like:
- how fast Sue could walk
- how well she could smell
- and that Sue might not be a girl
dinosaur, after all!

But there's still lots we don't know
about T. rex.

No one knows how long a
T. rex tail is. No skeleton has ever been
found with the whole tail in place. And
remember those titchy T. rex arms? They
were about the same size as your dad's,
but the muscles were twice as big!
Scientists know that:

- they couldn't help to catch anything

Stretch!

- they were too titchy to lift food to that great big T.rex mouth

Dribble!

- they couldn't act as legs for walking on all fours!

Oof!

They still don't know what T.rex *could* do with them! But there are new and amazing discoveries being made all the time. Maybe one day soon we'll know the answer.

Dinosaur expert Jack Horner has been working on a new dig in Hell Creek. His team have found five new T. rex skeletons. It will take a while to dig them out, but they already think one skeleton is even bigger than Sue!

So, even after millions and millions of years, T. rex is still king of the lizards. No wonder it always looks like it's smiling!

DINONEWS

YOUR DAY–TO–DAY DINO NEWS.

ALL NEW
T.REX FINDS

New dino find!
More terrifying than
T.rex?

**Was T.rex a great
big chicken?**

T.rex SHOCK
Hell Creek, Montana

STOP PRESS!
MORE TERRIFYING THAN T.REX?

Dinosaur experts in Argentina, South America, have dug up the biggest meat-eating dino EVER found. In fact, there are SIX skeletons in this great big dino graveyard.

Until now, experts weren't certain whether massive meat-eaters could really hunt in packs, but this find proves that they did.

The giant dino was bigger and heavier than T.rex but it had shorter, stumpier legs, and jaws that snapped shut like super-sharp scissors.

One expert says the beast, "...would have been terrifying!" Another reckons that meat-eaters couldn't have grown much bigger... Could they?

April 2000

WAS T.REX A GREAT BIG CHICKEN?

A fossil of a T.rex leg bone was found deep in the ground in Dakota, USA. But it was too heavy for the helicopter that collected it. Scientists were forced to break the bone in half – and they couldn't believe what they found inside...

Fossils are the hard parts of a creature that have turned to stone long after the flesh has rotted. But inside this fossil there were still some scraps of fleshy tissue!

WAS T.REX A GREAT BIG CHICKEN?

T.REX – MEAT-EATING MONSTER OR GRAIN-CHOMPING CHICKEN?

Lab tests compared cells from the flesh with cells from animals alive today.

The result? Scientists found that T.rex really is related to a chicken!

T.REX "MAY NOT BE KILLER" SHOCK

Still digging at his site in Hell Creek, Montana, T.rex expert Jack Horner, has now found fossil remains from at least eight T.rexes. The dig is changing his ideas about T.rex. Jack now says that:

- T.rex had a very stiff spine, so it couldn't move fast enough to hunt.

- It behaved more like a vulture than a lion. It hung around huge herds of veggie dinos, where food was easy to find.

- T.rex didn't need to kill. Instead it just waited for one huge dino to die and gobbled up as much as it could!

So if T.rex only ate animals that were already dead it wasn't a terrifying killer after all! Other experts, like Dr Witmer of Ohio University, disagree.

Dr Witmer has carried out tests that show:

• T.rex had really good hearing and balance
• its eyes moved quickly to follow its prey.

Dr Witmer says this information proves that T.rex was definitely a hunter and a killer.

So who's right and who's wrong? The argument rages on…

Di-yes/Di-no quiz

You've read the book so this quiz will be eea-sy! Just answer "di-yes" or "di-no" to each of these sentences:

1 T.rex was the biggest dinosaur EVER. Di-yes/Di-no

2 T.rex had long arms that it used for scratching its back. Di-yes/Di-no

3 T.rex had other creatures living in its jaws. Di-yes/Di-no

4 If a T.rex tooth broke it just grew another one. Di-yes/Di-no

5 T.rex was always hungry. Di-yes/Di-no

6 A baby T.rex had a fluffy coat. Di-yes/Di-no

7 A female T.rex was smaller than a male. Di-yes/Di-no

8 Edmontosaurus was very good at blowing up balloons. Di-yes/Di-no

9 T.rex was really good at seeing, hearing and smelling. Di-yes/Di-no

10 Triceratops could kill T.rex by stabbing the giant dino with its horns. Di-yes/Di-no

Answers

1 Oh di-no it wasn't! (See page 10)

2 Di-no it didn't (See pages 11 and 63)

3 Di-yes, it did! (See pages 26–27)

4 Di-yes, it did! (See page 28)

5 Di-no, it wasn't! (See page 37)

6 Di-yes, it did! (See pages 46–47)

7 Di-no, it wasn't! (See page 48)

8 Di-no, it wasn't! (See page 33)

9 Di-yes, that's true! (See pages 14–23)

10 Di-yes, it could! (See page 38)

How well do you know dinos?

Can you match each dino name with a sentence and a picture?

Edmontosaurus
T.rex
Triceratops
Parksosaurus
Pterosaur

This creature helped T.rex look after its teeth!

A veggie dino that couldn't fight back.

A nippy little dino that T.rex liked to eat.

A big scary meat eater.

A veggie dino that was good at fighting.

Answers

Edmontosaurus
A veggie dino that couldn't fight back.

T.rex
A big scary meat eater.

Triceratops
A veggie dino that was good at fighting.

Parksosaurus
A nippy little dino that T.rex liked to eat.

Pterosaur
This creature helped T.rex look after its teeth!

TERRIBLE T. wordsearch

```
S U R U A S O S K R A P R
U T I T C H Y A R M S Q L
R Z O R B K M R T J S T M
U S F J N W L V M P H R E
A E Y I R E N R O H E T A
S L T P Z D O T Y R A N T
O S N U X B A K L R D M E
N Y A P W R D N G E B T A
N P I L E E C H E S U P T
A R D C H W U L M F T R E
R Z I G Z A G R P A T S R
Y R E T H E L L C R E E K
T J L K R U A S O R E T P
```

HEAD-BUTT
HELL CREEK
HORNER
LEECHES
MEAT EATER
PARKSOSAURUS
PTEROSAUR

STINKY
TITCHY ARMS
TRICERATOPS
TYRANNOSAURUS
TYRANT
ZIG-ZAG

These thirteen words, or pairs of words, are hidden in the wordsearch. See if you can find them all. It's not easy! They might be written up, down, backwards, forwards or diagonally.

ANSWERS

S U R U A S O S K R A P R
T I T C H Y A R M S Q L
Z O R B K M R T J S T M
S F J N W L V M P H R E
E Y I R E N R O H E R A
L T P Z D O T Y R A N T
S N U X B A K L R D M E
Y A P W R D N G E B T A
P I L E E C H E S B U T
R D C H W U L M F T R E
Z I G Z A G R P A T T R
R E T H E L L C R E E K
J L K R U A S O R E T P

78

Index

arms 10–11, 45, 62, 72

babies 46–8, 50–1, 72
birds 68
brain 14–15
Brown, Barnum 59

calling 20–1, 33
chickens 67–8

eating 31–2, 37, 50, 55, 66–7
Edmontosaurus 32, 34, 36–7, 73–4, 76
eyes 16–18, 52, 56, 70

females 48, 73
fighting 55, 75–6
fossils 58, 66, 69

head 11, 13–16, 38, 40, 45
head-butting 54, 56
hearing 14–15, 20, 22, 70, 73
Hendrickson, Sue 60
herds 20, 32, 34–5, 38
Horner, Jack 64, 69
horns 38, 40, 56, 73
hunting 35, 65, 69, 71

jaws 13, 26, 36, 55, 67, 72

leaders 35, 48–9, 54
legs 11, 63, 66

males 48, 73
meat-eaters 10, 26, 28, 53, 65–7, 75–6

neck 15, 36, 55
nests 25
nose 22, 33, 56

Osborn, Henry Fairfield 59

packs 23, 25, 48, 52, 55, 65
Parksosaurus 41, 74, 74
Pterosaur 26, 74, 76

running 40, 43–4, 52

scientists 20, 58, 60–2, 66–8
seeing 14–15, 18, 22, 38, 73
skeletons 59–60, 62, 64–5
skull 15, 60
smelling (sniffing) 14–15, 22–3, 42, 61, 73

tail 11, 58, 62
teeth 13, 26, 28, 30, 34, 47, 53, 72, 75–6
Triceratops 38, 40–1, 73–4, 76

"These books ... provide a great deal of information in a highly accessible way using a small amount of easily read text imaginatively combined with plenty of line drawings ... a good choice for dinosaur fans who are also reluctant readers as well as those who are already enthusiastic." *Wordpool News*